MY VERY OWN BOOK OF

ROCKS & MINERALS

Designed by

_____

Rocks and minerals

Our world is made up of many different rocks and minerals. All rocks are made up of combinations of one or more minerals. A mineral is a chemical compound that occurs naturally. Minerals include precious stones and ores, which are minerals containing metals. Sometimes minerals form crystals. Deep heat inside the earth melts the minerals in rocks, which later cool and harden into new structures called crystals. Crystals are often transparent, with smooth, shiny surfaces.

Leaf imprint
A fossil is the remains of an animal or plant preserved naturally. While the soft parts of this leaf decayed, the hard parts became covered in mud. The shape was preserved when the mud hardened into rock over millions of years.

In the habit
The general shape of a crystal is called its habit. Studying the shape of a crystal helps identify it. Like most minerals, calcite occurs in groups of many crystals – these are called aggregates.

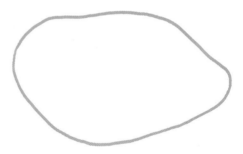

Prehistoric bug
In prehistoric times, the sticky resin of a tree trapped this bug. Over millions of years, the resin hardened into amber. Insects, spiders, and even frogs have been preserved this way.

Soft and slippery
Because raw talc is so soft, it can be easily scratched. It is greasy to the touch and has a pearly surface.

Sulfur
Yellow crystals form when molten sulfur cools. Large underground deposits in the United States provide sulfur for making rubber and chemicals.

Wiry metal

Today, silver is less valuable than gold or platinum. One of its main disadvantages is that it tarnishes easily. Silver is made into jewelry and ornaments and is widely used in the photographic industry.

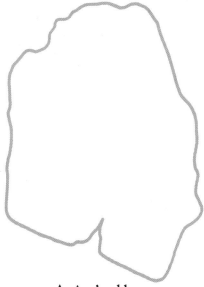

Artists' gold

Orpiment is not as valuable as real gold. Medieval artists used orpiment to imitate gold in their paintings.

Treasure rock

Before 1870, diamonds were only found as crystals or fragments in riverbeds. In the late 1800s, diamonds were discovered in kimberlite rock in South Africa.

Gold grains

Gold is produced from rounded grains that occur in some gravel and sand deposits. It has been used for coins, decoration, and jewelry for thousands of years.

Platinum

Most platinum minerals occur as very small grains in nickel deposits. Platinum was first noted in the 18th century, but it was not widely used until this century.

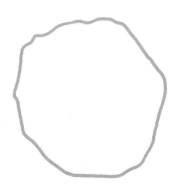

Opal fossil

Opal often replaces the tissues of wood and the bones and shells of ancient animals in a kind of fossilization.

Jewelry

Throughout the ages people have enjoyed collecting items of great beauty or value. Fine pieces of jewelry are carefully crafted from platinum, gold, or silver, and set with precious gems. Semiprecious stones and organic minerals, such as pearls and amber, also make stunning jewelry. Costume jewelry is often made from less valuable materials, such as shells or coral. Imitation gems are only made of glass.

Jet earrings
Jet is an organic mineral, formed from the remains of wood that was immersed in stagnant water millions of years ago. It is dense enough to be carved and polished and made into jewelry.

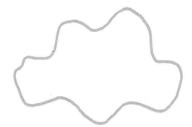

Cutting gems
Many gemstones look rather dull when they are mined. To produce a sparkling gem, a lapidary (gemstone expert) must cut and polish them to enhance their natural qualities.

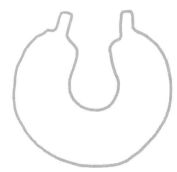

Golden beads
This gold collar dates back to the 16th century BC. It was decorated by a process called granulation. This is when gold wire is melted down to make tiny beads, which are then soldered to a surface.

Box brooch
Viking brooches were often lavishly decorated. But they were not just for show. Vikings wore brooches to hold their clothes in place. A wealthy woman wore this box brooch to fasten her cloak.

Silver cross
This silver cross is set with six sapphires and four other gemstones: an inky blue spinel, an amethyst, a citrine, and a brown zircon. Another sapphire sits at the top.

Aztec treasure
When a wealthy ancient South American died, his tomb would be filled with precious gold and silver objects.

Minerals

Azurite is a startlingly blue copper mineral

Dioptase is prized for its color, but it is rarely cut into gems because it is brittle and too soft to be worn

Wulfenite is usually an orange or yellow color, but it may also be brown, gray, or greenish-brown

Malachite produces a rich, bright green pigment used in paint

Polished smithsonite is used as a decorative stone

Clinoclase is dark greenish-blue to greenish-black in color, with a bluish-green streak

Crocoite is an orange-red color and has a hard, brittle surface

Rhodochrosite is sometimes cut into gems for collectors, but it is more commonly used as a decorative stone

Sulfur is often found in volcanic vents and blow-holes

Orpiment resembles gold

Talc is the softest mineral and is used to make talcum powder

CRYSTALS

The color of vanadinite
ranges from bright red to
brownish-red, brown, or yellow

Chryosprase is the most the
valuable of all the quartz crystals

This group of crystals
was found at Mont
St. Hilaire, Quebec

Bournonite is a well-
formed crystal and very rare

The different colors
on the surface of
hematite are very striking

Hemimorphite
has a silky surface

Fluorite occurs in a
great variety of colors

Rose quartz can be cut
as a precious stone or
used for carvings and beads

This collection of
calcite crystals looks
like scoops of ice cream

PRECIOUS METALS

Gold is a soft metal
that can be easily shaped

Pyrite can be used to
make costume jewelry

Apart from being used to
make jewelry, platinum is used
in oil refinery

Copper is used in
the electricity industry

Platinum is the rarest
and most valuable of
all the precious metals

This Viking brooch
glitters with gold and silver

This gold collar is
decorated with tiny gold beads

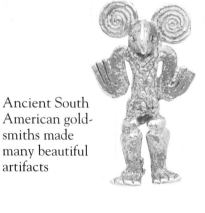

Ancient South
American gold-
smiths made
many beautiful
artifacts

This silver
goat is from
Persia and
dates back
to the 5th
century BC

In medieval times, silver
was more valuable than gold

This rock is
scattered with
real gold grains

PRECIOUS JEWELS

These diamonds are dull because they have been carried long distances in rough water with other rocks and gravel

The beauty and rarity of garnet makes it a valuable gem

The finest blue turquoise comes from Iran and has been used in decoration for 6,000 years

This diamond is embedded in a kind of volcanic rock called kimberlite

It was once believed that amethyst could cure drunkenness

The turquoise in this rock looks like a mosaic

Jade is tough enough to be cut into fancy designs

This Persian turquoise ornament is engraved and inlaid with gold

Turquoise was one of the very first gemstones to be mined

Crystal balls have been used for telling the future since Greek and Roman times

The bluish color of sapphire comes from tiny amounts of iron and titanium

GEMS AND GEMSTONES

The best moonstones come from Burma

Amethyst jewelry was very fashionable in the 19th century

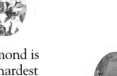

Aquamarine ranges from pale green to blue

Diamond is the hardest known mineral

Emerald is a brilliant green form of the mineral beryl

Yellow sapphire was once known as oriental topaz

Garnet is often cut into rounds or ovals with plain, curved surfaces

This fine gemstone weighs hundreds of carats

Pearls were once thought to be the tears of gods

This gold box is studded with 16 diamonds

The ancient Chinese believed that jade had the power to make a person live forever

This silver cross is set with eleven sparkling gemstones

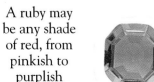

Pure corundum is found in Sri Lanka

Peridot, which contains iron, is a bottle-green color

Turquoise was thought to warn the wearer of danger by changing color

A ruby may be any shade of red, from pinkish to purplish

The markings on polished tiger eye are clearly striped

Peridot has been used in jewelry for thousands of years

The beauty of a sapphire is in its rich color

Most opal forms in sedimentary rocks

Topaz occurs in igneous rocks

FOSSILS

Jet is light to wear, making it especially suitable for earrings

Even though it is about 40 million years old, much of the original detail and texture of this beech leaf can still be seen

Some of the most common fossils are the shells of sea creatures called ammonites

This fossil of a poplar leaf is about 25 million years old, yet it is very similar to the poplar leaves of today

Amber is the fossil resin of extinct coniferous trees that lived millions of years ago

This insect is preserved inside amber

The shells of these ammonites are covered with iron pyrite, also known as "fool's gold"

This piece of wood is covered with opal

Growth rings tell us about the growth of a tree when it was living

These fossils are the delicate skeletons of corals

Rare and valuable

There are more than 3,000 species of minerals to choose from. But not all of them are objects of great value and beauty. Minerals have key qualities upon which they are judged and valued, such as their durability, hardness, and rarity. People like to collect gems with a difference – they may seek the rare color of a gem, or its exceptional size or shape.

Useful jade
The Spanish conquerors of Mexico wore amulets made from jade. They believed that jade prevented and cured hip and kidney complaints.

A rare sight
It is usual for gold to occur as fine grains scattered throughout a rock, or as invisible gold that cannot be seen by the naked eye. This group of crystals is therefore extremely rare.

Rose quartz crystal
Pink or peach-colored quartz is called rose quartz. Crystals of rose quartz are rare; more usually it is found as a massive lump.

Tricky platinum
Early jewelers had difficulty melting this precious metal. It was not until the 1920's that technology was developed to work it properly. Platinum is valuable because it does not tarnish easily.

What's it worth?
This magnificent crystal of spodumene is a collector's item because it is so fragile.

Color and light

Metals and other impurities produce various colors in minerals. For example, sapphires and rubies are varieties of a mineral called corundum. The presence of iron and titanium turns corundum blue to produce blue sapphires, and the presence of chromium turns corundum red to produce red rubies. These kinds of minerals are called allochromatic. But some minerals are nearly always the same color because of their atomic structure. These minerals are called idiochromatic.

Dioptase
Dioptase is a vivid green color with a hint of blue, prized by collectors for its beauty. It is sometimes confused with emerald.

Corundum
Pure corundum is colorless, but tiny amounts of impurities produce a wide variety of colors such as red, yellow, green, and blue.

Purple amethyst
The most highly prized form of quartz is amethyst. It often occurs in crystals large enough to be cut as gemstones.

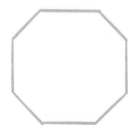

Peridot
Peridot is a gem variety of the mineral olivine, a magnesium and iron silicate that is common in volcanic rocks.

Ancient blue
By crushing colored rocks and mixing the powders with animal fats, early people made their own brightly colored paint. Azurite makes a bright, earthy blue paint.

True blue
The term sapphire on its own indicates a blue stone. This sapphire has grown together with crystals of hard, glassy spinel.

Yellow sapphire
Not all sapphires are blue. There are yellow sapphires and pink sapphires, and all are varieties of the mineral corundum.

Look closely
Tiger eye forms when tiny fibers of asbestos are replaced by quartz and iron oxides. If you look very closely at carved and polished tiger eye, you can see a likeness of a cat's eye.

Blue moon
Most moonstones have a blue or white sheen, rather like the light of the moon.

Blue mosaic
Turquoise occurs in nodules and veins of green or blue. Copper makes it blue, and iron makes it green.

Play of colors
The different colors on the surface of hematite are called a "play of colors." They resemble the different colors you see on a soapy bubble or oil film.

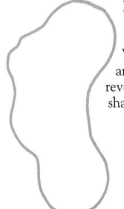

Malachite
Malachite is a copper mineral. When it is carved and polished, it reveals different shades of green.

Inca rose
Minerals that contain manganese, such as rhodochrosite, are normally pink or red. In Argentina, rhodochrosite is known as "Inca rose."

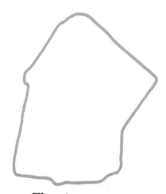

Fluorite
When exposed to ultraviolet light, fluorite gives out a visible light of many colors. This is called fluorescence.

Birthstones

Some cultures associate gems with the signs of the zodiac, and others associate them with the months of the year. In the ancient world, people believed that gems came from the heavens. In the 18th century, it became fashionable to wear your own birthstone jewelry. See if you can find the sticker of your own personal birthstone and stick it on your birthday month below.

January
Garnet

February
Amethyst

April
Diamond

May
Emerald

June
Pearl

March
Aquamarine

August
Peridot

September
Sapphire

October
Opal

July
Ruby

November
Topaz

December
Turquoise